OUR LITTLE DREAMS

Written by Alma Haley Green
Illustrated by Daria Riabets

A note from the author:

Thank you for purchasing my book!

I poured my heart into creating this book, with every page crafted to celebrate love, kindness, and the beauty of diversity. My hope is that it not only sparks joy and curiosity in your little ones, but also becomes a special part of your family's journey in embracing and appreciating what makes each of us unique. Through this story, I want to share a piece of that love with you, and I hope you'll like it.

With love, Alma

For all the children
of planet Earth
and their friends.

Look at the world,
Such a great big place
Full of people,
Each with a different face!

Different to look at,
Every single one,
And yet the same species
We call human.

All with different talents,
Likes and dreams
Made of different fabric
But with the same seams!

Emily is my friend.
She's funny and shy.
She's always there for me
When I need to cry.

She wants to be a policewoman
And protect those in need.
She's great at skateboarding.
You should see her speed!

Darren wants to be a poet and write all day.
He said he may even try to write a play!

He can make me laugh
When I'm feeling down,
No one is better
At undoing a frown!

Hassan wants to be a lawyer
Like his mother is.
He's amazingly clever,
A really smart wiz!

No one is better at sports,
Especially football,
And he will help his friends up
Whenever they fall.

Lashawna dreams of being a teacher
When she sleeps at night.
She wants to help children
Learn to read and write!

She loves rice noodles
With carrots and peas.
And playing with friends
Like Emily, Meggie and me.

Maggie loves animals
Big or tall or small.
She wants to be a vet
And take care of them all.

Kai longs to be an artist
And paint what's in his head.

He's sometimes a little messy
And doesn't make his bed.
He makes the best sandcastles
When we're at the beach,
And his all-time favorite food
Is a ripe, juicy peach

Franz has a fancy leg
He calls his super blade.
It only fits on him
Because it's specially made.

He loves to drink fizzy pop
From his favorite cup.
He's going to be a doctor
When he's all grown up.

Maddy has cool wheels
And can spin around so quick.
That I sometimes wonder
How she doesn't get sick.

Someday she'll be a great musician
And play a concert hall,
But, for now, she just enjoying
Her favorite season: fall!

Then of course there's little me,
And I don't know what exactly I want to be,

I guess I'll just wait a while and see,
Right now, I'm still working on A-B-C.

We all have different dreams, I guess,
But none of them are worth any more or less,

No, they're just different, and I think that's great.
Though dreams can change—after all, we're not even eight!

On the outside, we look different, too.
Eyes may be brown or green or even blue.

But we can still help each other
And have fun when we play,
And that's what really matters
At the end of the day!

Some of us are strong,
Some of us funny,
Some of us are gloomy,
And others are sunny.

Some are shy,
Others are bold,
Some are leaders,
And others prefer to be told.

The world is just like my group of friends here:
Different and the same—something we should hold dear.

Our differences make us who we are.
Each one of us is our own unique star.

We're different recipes
With different cooks.
We're a quilt of different dreams,
Loves and looks.

We're a mixture of colors
That makes everything bright
If we share our differences
With love and light!

Encourage kids to talk about diversity. Try to notice the beauty of diversity in nature and all things around. Discuss some questions below.

- What flowers do you know? Do you like flower gardens?
- What if there was only one type of flower? Or a few?
- Did you know that every snowflake is unique?
  It is what makes them so beautiful.
- And what about people, animals, plants?
- Do you think differences make the world better?
- What dreams do you have? And what dreams do your friends have?
- Who you want to be? And what about your friends?
- What food do you like? And what food do your friends like?
  Do you have the food you both like?
- What common features do you have with your friends?
  What differences do you have?
- What is the most beautiful about you? And about them?
- What do you think diversity is?

Ask if your kids have some other questions. Be patient with their answers. And show on your own attitude the value of diversity.